WEDDING PHOTOGRAPH
GOES HERE

THIS JOURNAL BELONGS TO:

_____

_____

MY WEDDING JOURNAL

RYLAND PETERS & SMALL
LONDON • NEW YORK

HOW I KNEW HE
WAS THE ONE

THE STORY OF US

The best friend will probably acquire the best spouse, because a good marriage is founded on the talent for friendship.

Friedrich Nietzsche (1844–1900),
from *Friendship and Marriage*

HOW WE MET

Where we met

_____
_____
_____
_____
_____
_____
_____
_____

First impressions

_____
_____
_____
_____
_____
_____
_____
_____

How we felt about each other

_____
_____
_____
_____
_____
_____

OUR FIRST DATE

Where we went
_____
_____
_____
_____

What I wore
_____
_____
_____

What he wore
_____
_____
_____

Memorable moments
_____
_____
_____
_____
_____
_____
_____
_____

THE PROPOSAL

Where we were
_____
_____
_____
_____
_____
_____
_____
_____

How I felt
_____
_____
_____
_____
_____
_____
_____
_____
_____
_____

How we celebrated
_____
_____
_____
_____
_____
_____
_____
_____
_____

OUR ENGAGEMENT

How long our engagement lasted

_____

_____

_____

_____

_____

How we felt

_____

_____

_____

_____

_____

_____

_____

_____

_____

_____

_____

_____

_____

THE ANNOUNCEMENT

Who we told first

_____
_____
_____
_____
_____

How they reacted

_____
_____
_____
_____
_____

What they asked

_____
_____
_____
_____
_____

How we felt

_____
_____
_____
_____

OUR ENGAGEMENT PARTY

Where it was held

When it was held

Most moving moment

Funniest moment

ENGAGEMENT PARTY
INVITATION

ENGAGEMENT PARTY
PHOTO

THE PREPARATIONS

The heart wants what it wants.
There's no logic to these things.
You meet someone and you fall
in love and that's that.

Woody Allen (1935–)

THE GUESTLIST

Who we invited

THE INVITATIONS

The style

Who designed them

The reaction

THE BRIDAL SHOWER

Who I invited

_____
_____
_____
_____
_____
_____
_____
_____

What we did

_____
_____
_____
_____
_____
_____
_____

The gifts I was given

_____
_____
_____
_____
_____
_____

MY BACHELORETTE PARTY

Who I invited
_____
_____
_____
_____
_____

Where we went
_____
_____
_____
_____
_____

Most outrageous moment
_____
_____
_____
_____
_____

Most sentimental moment
_____
_____
_____
_____

HIS BACHELOR PARTY

Who he invited

Where they went

Funniest story recounted

OUR BRIDAL PARTY

The supreme happiness in life is the assurance of being loved for oneself, even in spite of oneself.

Victor Hugo (1802–1855), from *Les Misérables*

MY MATRON OF HONOR

Why I chose her
_____
_____
_____
_____
_____
_____

How she helped me
_____
_____
_____
_____
_____
_____

What she wore
_____
_____
_____

How she felt
_____
_____
_____

THE BEST MAN

Why he was chosen

How he helped at the wedding

What he wore

How he felt

THE BRIDESMAIDS

Who they were
_____
_____
_____
_____
_____

How they helped
_____
_____
_____
_____
_____

What they wore
_____
_____
_____
_____
_____

How they felt
_____
_____
_____
_____
_____

THE GROOMSMEN

Who they were

How they helped

What they wore

How they felt

FLOWER GIRLS

Who they were

How they helped

What they wore

How they felt

RINGBEARERS

Who they were

How they helped

What they wore

How they felt

THE REHEARSAL DINNER

Where we went
_____
_____
_____
_____
_____

Who we invited
_____
_____
_____
_____
_____

What we ate and drank
_____
_____
_____
_____
_____

How we felt
_____
_____
_____
_____
_____

THE BEAUTIFUL BRIDE

Marriage is the highest state of friendship. If happy, it lessens our cares by dividing them, at the same time that it doubles our pleasures by mutual participation.

Samuel Richardson (1689–1761), from *Clarissa*

MY WEDDING DRESS

Choosing my dress
_____
_____
_____
_____
_____
_____

The designer
_____
_____
_____
_____
_____

The fitting
_____
_____
_____
_____
_____

How I felt
_____
_____
_____
_____
_____

MY ACCESSORIES

Choosing my accessories

_____
_____
_____
_____
_____

My headwear

_____
_____
_____
_____

My shoes

_____
_____
_____
_____

My jewelry

_____
_____
_____
_____

Other accessories

_____
_____
_____
_____

MY BOUQUET

Choosing my bouquet

_____
_____
_____
_____
_____
_____

The flowers

_____
_____
_____
_____

The colors

_____
_____
_____
_____

How I felt

_____
_____
_____
_____
_____

MY HAIR AND MAKEUP

My beauty helpers

My hair

My makeup

My nails

THE CEREMONY

Of all serious things, marriage is the funniest.

Pierre De Beaumarchais (1732–1799),
from *The Marriage of Figaro*

THE CEREMONY VENUE

The location

_____
_____
_____
_____
_____
_____
_____

How we chose

_____
_____
_____
_____
_____
_____

The decoration

_____
_____
_____
_____

How I felt

_____
_____
_____
_____

THE FLOWERS

The flowers we chose

_____

_____

_____

_____

_____

Where they were arranged

_____

_____

_____

_____

_____

What they symbolize

_____

_____

_____

_____

_____

Where we placed them

_____

_____

_____

_____

THE ORDER OF SERVICE

The program of the ceremony

VOWS TO EACH OTHER

Our vows
_____
_____
_____
_____
_____
_____
_____
_____
_____
_____
_____
_____
_____
_____
_____
_____
_____
_____
_____
_____
_____
_____
_____
_____
_____
_____
_____

THE MUSIC

What was played

_____
_____
_____
_____
_____

How we chose the music

_____
_____
_____
_____
_____
_____
_____

How we felt

_____
_____
_____
_____
_____
_____

THE RINGS

The style of our rings
_____
_____
_____
_____
_____
_____
_____

Why we chose them
_____
_____
_____
_____
_____
_____
_____

How we felt when they were exchanged
_____
_____
_____
_____
_____
_____

THE RECEPTION

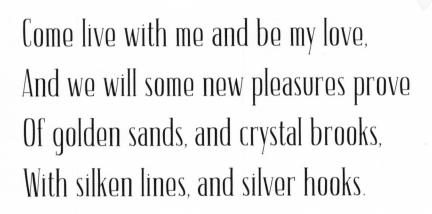

Come live with me and be my love,
And we will some new pleasures prove
Of golden sands, and crystal brooks,
With silken lines, and silver hooks.

John Donne (1572–1631), from *The Bait*

THE RECEPTION VENUE

The location
_____
_____
_____
_____
_____
_____
_____

How we chose
_____
_____
_____
_____
_____
_____

The decorations
_____
_____
_____
_____
_____
_____
_____
_____

THE SEATING PLAN

ATTACH SEATING
PLAN HERE

TABLE SETTINGS

Theme

Place cards

Centerpieces

Crockery and china

WEDDING FAVORS

The design

_____
_____
_____
_____
_____
_____

What we gave to our guests

_____
_____
_____
_____

How we chose the favors

_____
_____
_____
_____

Who made them

_____
_____
_____
_____

THE WEDDING MENU

ATTACH WEDDING
MENU HERE

OUR WEDDING CAKE

Who made the cake
_____
_____
_____
_____
_____
_____

The cake we chose
_____
_____
_____
_____
_____

Cake decoration
_____
_____
_____
_____

Cutting the cake
_____
_____
_____
_____

THE PLAYLIST AND PERFORMERS

Who performed at the wedding

_____

_____

_____

_____

_____

_____

Music during dinner

_____

_____

_____

_____

Evening playlist

_____

_____

_____

_____

Memorable moments

_____

_____

_____

_____

OUR FIRST DANCE

What we danced to

_____
_____
_____
_____
_____
_____

How we chose the song

_____
_____
_____
_____
_____
_____

How we felt

_____
_____
_____
_____
_____

Who followed us on the dancefloor

_____
_____
_____
_____
_____

SPEECHES & TOASTS

Who spoke
_____
_____
_____
_____
_____

What they said
_____
_____
_____
_____

Favorite quotes
_____
_____
_____

Memorable moments
_____
_____
_____
_____

OUR LASTING MEMORIES

Whatever our souls are made of,
his and mine are the same.

Emily Brontë (1818–1848),
from *Wuthering Heights*

MEMORIES OF THE DAY

My favorite moment

_____
_____
_____
_____
_____
_____

Most tearful moment

_____
_____
_____
_____
_____
_____

Happiest moment

_____
_____
_____

Funniest moment

_____
_____
_____

THE HONEYMOON

Where we went

How we chose where to go

What we did on our honeymoon

Our plans for the future

PHOTO ALBUM

Designer Maria Lee-Warren
Editor Miriam Catley
Production Manager Toby Marshall
Art director Leslie Harrington
Editorial director Julia Charles

Styling Selina Lake
All photography by Ali Allen, except:
Pages 6, 12, 29, 89, 94, 112 by Sussie Bell
Page 16 © Tim Hale Photography/Corbis
Page 33 by Catherine Gratwicke (The Linen Shed,
    boutique B&B near Whitstable, Kent, UK
    www.linenshed.com)
Page 44 by Tara Fisher
Pages 4, 34, 47, 66 (the home of Ros Fairman in
    London), 90, 93, 98, 111, by Debi Treloar
Page 105 by William Lingwood
Page 106 by www.johndayphotography.net
Page 143 by Polly Wreford
'Our Lasting Memories' divider by Sussie Bell
'The Ceremony' divider by Paul Massey

First published in 2013
by Ryland Peters & Small
20–21 Jockey's Fields
London WC1R 4BW
and
519 Broadway, 5th Floor
New York, NY 10012
www.rylandpeters.com

10 9 8 7 6 5 4 3 2 1

ISBN: 978-1-84975-447-7

Printed and bound in China

With very special thanks to:
www.pipii.co.uk
www.talkingtables.co.uk
www.davidaustinroses.com
www.gilfox.com
www.thepeopleshop.co.uk